MANIPULATION

TECHNIQUES IN DARK PSYCHOLOGY, INFLUENCING PEOPLE WITH PERSUASION, NLP, AND MIND CONTROL

EDWARD BENEDICT

INTRODUCTION

Manipulation is the conscious act of causing someone to do a certain thing or act in a certain way. Manipulation is clever, skillful, and sometimes unscrupulous. Manipulation is not always a bad thing. The clay bowl created in an art class was made from clay that was manipulated by someone's hands. The doctor put the broken bone back into place by using manipulation. The snowman was built by the hands of children who manipulated the snow into place.

Sometimes, manipulation is a bad thing. People can be manipulated to do things they would not usually do. Spouses manipulate each other. Parents manipulate children. And supervisors manipulate employees. People who manipulate others often act as though they have only the best interests in mind for the other person. They use caring as a disguise in getting what they really want, no matter what the other person wants. People who manipulate others in a negative way are usually known by an uncomplimentary term, such as sociopath or narcissist.

Knowing that manipulation is happening is the first step towards ending it. By knowing the signs of manipulation, people can often stop it before it becomes a bad habit or a detrimental way of life. Understanding how manipulation works is the key to controlling it and eliminating it.

MANIPULATING THE MIND
THROUGH NLP

Manipulation has come to carry a negative meaning but that is not necessarily true in all cases. Manipulation merely means to shape or mold something to a new, more desirable shape. Snow can be manipulated into the shape of a snowman. Clay can be manipulated into almost any shape. Small children being taught to take turns when playing and to use their manners are, in a sense, being manipulated by their parents. So manipulation is not always a negative event.

Using manipulation to control the mind of another person is powerful and fascinating. Since the mind is the key to everything a human being does, the ability to control that mind gives multitudes of power and ability. Techniques used to control the mind work because they take control of the thoughts a person has. These techniques are based primarily on the method of Neuro-Linguistic Programming (NLP). Using NLP makes it possible to control other people's minds using specific patterns and strategies.

. . .

THE HUMAN MIND works in a specific way. It looks for cause and effect. The mind creates an event in response to a stimulus it has received. Sometimes doctors use a test called an electroencephalogram to measure the actual physical working of the brain in order to look for patterns of activity that are associated with certain diseases and conditions, such as epilepsy. The two brain states most often studied are the alpha state and the beta state. The beta state is a high-function, active state. The alpha state has much lower frequencies than the beta state. It is the place where the mind experiences calmness and peacefulness. This state is very important because it is the state psychologists and hypnotists use for programming the mind, simply because this state carries fewer thought patterns than any other state in the brain.

THE TECHNIQUES USED in NLP enable the person doing the programming to introduce thoughts into another person's mind when it is unconscious that the person will not necessarily be aware of when conscious. The power of persuasion in NLP makes it a strong technique that is often used in fields such as marketing, politics, and the business world. Signals are used to convey thoughts into the unconscious mind that will influence the mind when the person is conscious.

SKILLED PROFESSIONALS who regularly use NLP to control other people know that the mind can be programmed to do amazing things if the person will allow it to happen. Often, people are resistant to this type of control because they are afraid of what might happen. There are countless jokes about a hypnotist making someone bark like a dog at a certain stimulus when they are awake. That is possible. But NLP has many good, positive uses.

· · ·

THE MAIN OBJECTIVE of NLP is to bring about inner changes in the way people see the world. It creates mental changes in the way events are perceived and teaches ways to engage in communication that is more responsible. It helps people make choices for more effectively responding or communicating in a given situation. It does not matter if the situation is of a professional or personal nature. These techniques enable the person to make better choices and also to feel empowered to carry out the choices.

SOMEONE TAKING advantage of the power of NLP will experience techniques similar to those used in hypnosis. During a therapy session, the person will be placed into a deep state of relaxation so that they are able to access the deepest section of their mind where unconscious thought is formed. They are then led on a mental quest through years of accumulated thoughts and beliefs. The ultimate goal is to access the experience from childhood that caused a particular pattern of behavior. The theory behind NLP is that all people carry all the resources needed to make positive life changes in their own minds. NLP merely gives them access to this information and gives them the techniques to use to make needed changes.

THE THERAPIST DOES NOT EVEN NEED to know about the problem that the person wishes to address. Techniques can be taught that will enable the person to make the necessary corrections without the therapist ever knowing what the actual problem is.

THE THERAPY TECHNIQUES in NLP act on the theory that all humans are perfect creations of nature. NLP therapists use this belief to teach people how to access their own sensory abilities and how to use these abilities to act on a particular stimulus or event. NLP practitioners also believe it is possible to teach the mind how to control the body to eliminate certain diseases.

The techniques used in NLP are not invasive and do not involve the use of medication. NLP can help with ways to increase self-esteem, correct destructive patterns and behaviors in personal relationships, improve the personal level of self-confidence, and are better able to cope with events that cause anxiety. There are many different techniques that NLP practitioners use to enable people to use these methods effectively.

NLP CAN BE USED to treat simple cases of Post-Traumatic Stress Disorder (PTSD). With PTSD, the person has experienced a traumatic event and that they experience stressful reactions when they encounter an event similar to the original traumatic event. This technique involves taking the person mentally through the event from beginning to end, reliving it in the mind as closely as possible. Then the therapist takes the patient through the event again, but this time from the end to the beginning. The idea is to take the person back to a safe place from the traumatic event so that when recurring events happen the mind automatically goes to the safe place and not the reaction place.

A METHOD for treating anxiety is a process that teaches the person to mentally track the physical path of the symptoms the feeling causes in the body. The patient is taught to think of an event that would cause feelings of anxiety. Then the patient is told to mentally follow the track of the physical response. For example, the physical response might begin in the stomach, travel to the chest, and then go down through the arms. Once the path is traced, the patient then turns their attention to the actual shape the feeling takes as it travels through the body. What size is the shape? Does it have a particular color? By totally understanding what the feeling looks like, the patient is able to reduce some of the power the shape holds. Then the patient is instructed to feel which way the feeling turns as it comes up through the body. Does it turn clockwise or counterclockwise? By determining the direction of the spiral the patient is then taught to turn the feeling in the other direction, effectively unwinding it and removing its source of power. The patient is also instructed to change the shape and color of the feeling, changing it to something more pleasant.

NLP can be used to effectively to change problem behaviors or emotions into positive ones. One process used provides a transformation process for the very core of the person. This process is highly client involved because the client personally addresses the problem mentally. The first step is for the person to ask the negative feeling what its intention is, and what it hopes to gain if it gets what it wants. Then the patient asks the feeling what its secondary desire is to achieve, once it gains its first desire. The patient continues in this vein until it reaches an answer that is based on emotion, such as happiness or peace, instead of a behavior or a thing. Once the end result is revealed, the patient then instructs the problem to automatically look for the pleasant emotion first, bypassing all other steps. Then the event that triggered the negative reaction originally will now cause a positive reaction.

ANOTHER POPULAR NLP process is feedback. Sometimes, this is referred to as biofeedback, especially when it is used in a medical setting. The basis of this technique lies in the idea that there will not be a failure but that the feedback will be successful. The idea is that a successful outcome will not be instantaneous but will be the result of a constantly repeating loop from the feedback. The lack of immediate success is viewed as a flaw in the feedback and not an immediate failure. This requires a feeling of ultimate faith in the process which is sometimes difficult, but it is necessary for success.

THIS METHOD WAS CREATED to change the beliefs that cause humans to see limits to their personal capabilities. This method runs under the assumption that multiple sensory experiences gather together to form a body of experience much like an emotional molecule. Revisiting the experience usually gives the person a mental picture of the event in great detail, feelings and emotions that were mentally gathered during the event, and messages gathered from others. Anything that has formed an attachment to the memory is examined in great detail. Then these attachments are examined, one by one, taken separately from one another. This removes the power from the memory group as a whole because each individual part of the memory has no power on its own. Then the mind is taught to use individual parts to create a new memory molecule that is made up of the remembrances the person chooses.

ANOTHER POPULARLY USED method is anchoring. This method employs the use of different colored paper circles that the patient uses to move from one event to another. The first circle is used to recall the unwanted stimulus and the particular event that leads to it. The other colored circles are used to represent a different, happier feeling. Thus the patient is taught to stand on the original circle to recall the unwanted emotion, and then move to another circle in order to replace the negative emotion with positive emotion. Once the emotion is changed to a positive one, the patient then returns to the original circle. The idea is to replace the negative emotions the event evokes with a new, more positive emotion.

ONE METHOD that has shown success in relieving the physical effects of anxiety and insomnia is to follow the feeling. Using this technique the patient begins by relaxing deeply. Then the patient is instructed to name where the feeling is placed in the body. This will be uncomfortable but it is necessary for the patient to know exactly where the feeling is and to acknowledge its presence. The patient is told to just feel it but not interact with it. Then the patient is told to ask questions of the feeling. Ask the feeling what it needs to help it leave the body. Take note of the first thought that comes into the mind. Check to see if the feeling is still present. If it is, then ask the feeling the question again. Keep accepting the feeling while questioning it. Keep asking the same question until no more answers come and the feeling is gone.

NLP MAY SEEM to have its basis in something dark and mysterious, but it really does not. NLP is nothing more than a method to use to teach the mind how to release the control that negative events have on the physical well-being and emotional state of the person. Think of the mind as a series of pathways. Every habit a person indulges in has its own pathway in the brain. When a stimulus occurs—something seen, heard, smelled, or remembered—a message is sent to a particular spot in the brain along a particular pathway. This is the spot that holds the memory for the reaction the mind has decided is appropriate for this stimulus. If a person sees their favorite cake they experience hunger. This is the mind's response to the stimulus the body received. So pathways can be created from good and bad experiences. The purpose of NLP is to reroute the pathways of negative stimuli and change the reaction to something pleasant and not something harmful or negative. In this way, NLP can be used for great benefits to people.

THE POWER OF PERSUASION

The power of persuasion means nothing more than using mental abilities to form words and feelings used to convince other people to do things they may or may not want to do. Some people are better able to persuade than other people. And some people are easier to persuade then other people.

The ease of persuading other people is directly tied to their current mental or emotional state. Someone who is lonely or tired is easier to persuade, simply because their defenses are lowered. Someone who is momentarily needy may be easier to persuade than someone who has a strong sense of self-worth. People who are at a low point in their lives are easy prey for others who might try to persuade them to do something they might not usually do.

Think of the publicity surrounding religious cults in the past. Everyone wanted to know how someone could fall prey to the teachings and ideals of the cult. The answer is simple: the victim was seeking something the cult offered. Whether the dangling carrot was food and shelter or love or religious freedom, the cult offers something tangible to the person who feels their life is lacking something important. And the person who joins the cult does not see themselves as a victim, but a participant. Think back further to the flower children of the sixties and seventies. These people lived in communes where everyone had a particular role to play. Some people would grow gardens to feed the members of the commune while others might wash laundry or clean houses. Everyone helped everyone else. The idea behind living in a commune was to leave behind the trappings that 'society' deemed as markers of success, such as fat paychecks and huge houses. These people wanted to live simply and enjoy what love and Mother Nature had to offer.

For every good group that assembles for the good of the people and works to help its members, there are countless groups that are brought together by forces that have no desire other than controlling other people for their own good. These leaders are very charismatic and very dangerous, because a person who is temporarily weak in mind or in the soul may not be able to resist their promises. It is important for everyone to understand how persuasion works in order to be able to resist it when needed.

The first step in persuasion involves the idea of reciprocating. If a person does something nice for someone else, then the receiving person usually feels the need to do something good in return. If someone helps their elderly neighbor carry in groceries from the car, that neighbor might feel obligated to bake homemade cookies for that person. A coworker who helps complete a project is more likely to receive assistance when it is needed. Many people do nice things for others all the time without expecting anything in return. The person who does nice things for people and then mentions some little favor that can be done in return may be someone to watch closely.

Nonprofit organizations use this tactic to gain more contributions to their causes. They will often send some little trinket or gift to prompt people to donate larger sums of money, or even just to donate where they might not have originally. The idea behind this is that the person opening the letter has received a little gift for no reason, so they might feel obligated to give something in return.

The consistency of self is the next step. People who commit to something, through verbal or written methods, are more likely to follow through on the idea that someone who makes no promises, Even if the original motivation is gone or the original incentive was taken away, people see this promise as being part of their image. They made a promise. This is often why counselors tell people to write their goals down. People are more likely to follow a written list they can refer to daily.

It is easy enough to change someone's image of themselves, especially if that person is needy or mentally weak. During times of war, it is customary to get prisoners to denounce their own country in order to hopefully turn others against that country. This is easy enough to do when starved prisoners are also mentally weak and have few defenses to use to deflect their captors. By constantly repeating statements that denounce the home country the captive begins to believe what they are saying because it must be true because they are saying it.

Another thing to be careful of is what is known as the herd mentality. Humans live in groups. Most of us want to belong to the herd and want to enjoy the safety being in a herd brings. Monkey see, monkey do. People tend to mirror the behavior seen around them. Think of the story of the emperor that runs around with no clothes on. His tailors had him convinced he was wearing fine garments, so he convinced all the people of his kingdom. And because they could not question the king, they had to believe what he was saying. This can also work in seriously negative ways. Think of the mob mentality. This is just another way to follow the herd, but it usually involves illegal or dangerous activities engaged in only because someone else was doing the same thing.

Some people are automatically tempted to follow authority. People in positions of authority can command blind respect to their authority simply by acting a certain way or putting on a uniform. The problem with this is that authority figures or those that look like authority figures, can cause some people to do extraordinary things they would not normally do had a person in a position of authority not been the one asking. And it is not simply held to people in uniform. People who carry themselves a certain way or speak a certain way can give the impression that they are something they are not.

For someone or something to be considered a credible authority, it must be familiar and people must have trust in the person or organization. Someone who knows all there is to know about a subject is considered an expert and is more likely to be trusted than someone who has limited knowledge of the subject. But the information must also make sense to the people hearing it. If there is not some semblance of accuracy and intelligence then the authority figure loses credibility. Even the person who is acknowledged as an expert will lack persuasive abilities if they are seen as not being trustworthy.

People want to be liked. People want to like other people. The problem is when some people use this fact to cause other people to do things they might not ordinarily do. People who are easy to like usually come across as very persuasive. People want to believe them. Con artists are extremely likeable people. The problem is that even likeable people may not have your personal best interests at heart. In fact, they probably only have their own interest in mind. Even someone who is totally legitimate, like a salesperson, is really most interested in their own interests. They may want their customer to be perfectly happy with their purchase so they will recommend that salesperson to their friends, but their ultimate concern is with themselves and their sales goals.

The worst part of the power that goes along with persuasion is that things that are scarce or hard to get are seen as much more valuable. People value diamonds because they are expensive and beautiful. If they were merely pretty stones, they would not be as interesting. Inconsistent rewards are a lot more interesting than consistent rewards. If a cookie falls every time a person rings a bell, then they are less likely to spend a lot of time ringing the bell because they know the cookie reward will always appear. If, however, the cookie only appears sometimes, people will spend much more time ringing the bell just in case this is the time the cookie will fall.

There are ways to improve the power of persuasion. Just like any other trait, it can be made stronger by following a few strategies and by regular practice.

Never hesitate to ask others what they think. Usually, those in a position of authority will not look for advice from other people. This is an opportunity many leaders neglect to take advantage of. Instead of asking others for their opinion and ideas, they miss the chance to make everyone feel like part of the group with an equal role to play. Besides, leaders who are not afraid to ask for input from others might learn something they did not know before.

Always remember to ask for advice, not feedback. People love being asked to give advice. Asking for feedback means that an opinion has already been given and the speaker wants to know what everyone else thinks of their own opinion. In many situations, there will be no responses because no one wants to disagree or be seen as argumentative, particularly with an authority figure. But asking for advice gives people a chance to voice their own opinions.

Before asking for any type of assistance, set the stage. People do not like being put on the spot. Walking up to someone and immediately asking for a favor sends two messages. The first one is that the favor is more important than the person. In this case, the favor needed is the focus of the conversation. Say that Bob walks into the room, goes straight up to Bill and asks Bill to assist at a fundraiser that weekend. Bill is caught off guard and must make an immediate decision. Does he say no, in front of others, and look like a mean-spirited person for not helping at the fundraiser? Or does he answer with yes without really knowing if he wants to do it or not? Whichever way the conversation goes, when Bill looks back on it later he may wonder if Bill even considers him a friend or if he just comes around when he wants help with something.

Now if Bob had bothered to set the stage for asking for the favor, he would have approached the conversation in a totally different manner. First, he would have approached Bill with a friendly greeting and cheerful smile. He would take a few minutes to make small talk with Bill, perhaps asking about his work life or his family life. After chatting cheerfully for a few minutes Bob would approach the idea of the fundraiser in a casual manner. "Hey, Bill, by the way...." He would explain what he needed Bill to do, explain how much he would really enjoy having Bill's presence at the fundraiser, then asking Bill to get back with him as soon as possible with an answer. He would assure Bill that whatever decision he made would be fine, although he really hoped Bill would be able to join him.

What is the difference between the two situations? In the second situation, Bill feels wanted. He feels needed. He feels as though his presence, or the lack of it, is important to Bob. In the second situation, Bob is most likely to get an honest answer. And what if Bill is not able to help Bob at the fundraiser? Bill will be more likely to help Bob in the future because he not only feels valued but he feels like he owes Bob something, Bill would probably be thinking that he owed Bob one in the future.

Persuasion is a powerful tool in the game of life. Persuasive people know that they have an amazing power, and they know how to use it correctly. They know how to listen and really hear what other people have to say. They are very good at making a connection with other people, and this makes them seem even more honest and friendly. They make others feel that they are knowledgeable and can offer a certain sense of satisfaction. They also know when to momentarily retreat and regroup. They are not pushy. They are persuasive.

DEFINING DESIRED OUTCOMES

The idea behind being a persuasive person, the main objective of persuasion, is to get something in return. There is no sense in practicing the art of persuasion if there is nothing desired in return. Persuasion means to cause someone to do something specific. Therefore, some sort of gain is desired, some sort of end result.

In order to know the intended end result of the persuasive effort, there must be a defined desired outcome. The person doing the persuading wants something tangible, something definable. But what do they want? Well, that is completely up to them to decide. But they must decide, before engaging in any form of persuasion, exactly what they hope to achieve at the end of the conversation.

This is what is meant as defining desired outcomes. The thing that is desired must be decided before any kind of persuasive tactics begin so that the person doing the persuading understands the desired outcome.

Pretend the office is holding a meeting to decide the location of a new office. The old office is small and cramped. The business is growing and needs more room to be able to continue to grow. So an office meeting will take place where, hopefully, the new location will be decided upon. This is the first step in defining the desired outcome, knowing what the proposed outcome is. In this case, it is the location of the new office.

So the meeting has been set for a particular time and place. Finished, right? Wrong. Without some sort of order and organization, the meeting will be unproductive and the desired outcome probably will not happen. The meeting is crucial to the desired outcome. Without some sort of specific plan then the meeting is nothing more than people in an office meeting in one room to make conversation.

So now it is necessary to set up the meeting; to have a plan as to how the meeting will proceed. Since this is a meeting of the entire office, there is no need to decide who to invite since everyone will be in attendance. So the next step is to create the agenda for the meeting. Will there be time for questions? Will certain people be invited to participate by offering specific recommendations for the new location? How will the ultimate decision be reached? All these factors need to be decided before the meeting begins.

When beginning the meeting be sure to mention the desired outcome. Let everyone know exactly what they are there to discuss. Make sure everyone involved knows and understand the desired outcome. Set a specific time for discussion and a time when the decision will be made. Then when the meeting is reaching the end of its prescribed time restate the objective and determine if a decision can be made or if more research is needed.

An outcome is nothing more than an end result that can be seen and measures. It is the consequence of the action. It is the conclusion that comes from persuading someone to do something. In any desired outcome there are four things that will need to be decided before the desired outcome can be decided upon. Those four things are: is something specific desired, is something already owned needing to be kept, who should be connected with and how, and what skills are needed to achieve the desired outcome.

It is important to decide these things because the underlying objectives will definitely affect the way the outcome is to be gained. It is similar to a football game where there is a defensive team and an offensive team. One group attacks the opposing team and one group defends against the attacks from the opposing teams. Each team will have a different set of priorities and procedures. Their desired outcomes will be quite different from one another. Each team will need to decide what it is they want to learn, defend, or acquire. The goal will determine the game plan.

The goal is the desired outcome. Behind any goal and its desired outcome is the need for change. Some sort of change needed has been identified and will be achieved. The path to achievement begins with setting a goal. The end of this journey is the desired outcome. It is necessary to understand that these are two separate entities that work together to achieve a result.

A goal is a destination. An outcome is a specific thing; it can be seen and measured. While setting the goal is vital to receiving the outcome, they are two quite different things and should be treated as such.

Goals always have reasons behind them. Something that is thought of as being necessary to happiness, to wealth, to health, or just because it is truly desired, is just not there. Whatever the reason is, it is that exact reason that drives forward progress toward the desired outcome. In order to be able to progress, to go forward to the goal, that goal and the idea of achieving it must be firmly entrenched in your mind. Without a steady focus on the goal, there is no possibility that the goal will ever be reached.

Imagine going to work every day for fifteen years, doing the same job every day. Imagine this is a job that needed college courses, so it was a chosen job. During the past fifteen years, doing the same job every day has been rewarding and profitable. There have been several promotions, the last of which came with a private secretary and a lovely large office. Several other people, who have not been working here quite as long, are now the team that directly reports every Monday in this large new office.

But going to work has become somewhat boring. The job just

does not bring the amount of satisfaction it once did. The problem is not in the job itself but in the person doing the job. What seemed so right all those years ago now feels so wrong. What is really desired is more interaction with people. In managing other people, a new skill has emerged: the ability to take raw recruits and mold them into productive team members with a bright future. That is the job that brings happiness and satisfaction.

But while this thought has been firmly entrenched in the mind for months now, no changes have been made to get closer to the goal of that type of occupation. And so every Monday morning is filled with team meetings, every day is filled with spreadsheets, and every Friday is filled with boundless joy that another work week has passed. Why?

The answer to *Why?* Is procrastination. Whether intentional or unintentional, procrastination has ruined many good intentions. Unintentional procrastination does happen sometimes. Everyone has that moment of "oops, I meant to take care of that today I'll get to it first thing in the morning." That is unintentional; something was forgotten. Intentional procrastination means knowing something needs to be done but putting it off until whenever. Many people do this with dreams and desires, especially those that will require extra work to accomplish or simply just a big leap of faith. Changing careers when one is firmly established is a scary thing. But what someone wants at twenty is not necessarily what they want at forty. People change. Their hearts change. They must be willing to follow their dreams and make them a reality. But people procrastinate out of fear.

So ask these three questions:

1. What exactly am I afraid of? Do I fear to lose a great job that will pay for my kid's college and not being able to find one that pays as well? What if I have to take a pay cut and can no longer pay the mortgage? What happens if I lose my health insurance? These are all valid question

that must be addressed when considering a large change in employment.

2. What will I gain if I am able to conquer this fear? What great gain will be realized? Will it be a new job, a new career that is more in line with current life goals? Maybe the real dream is the chance to help other people.

3. What do I do to fight this fear? Accept the fear as real. Acknowledge its existence. Then make a plan to reach the new goal and proceed without waiting. Go forward without procrastination.

Now, it is time to set a goal to make this dream a reality. Identify the goal as specifically as possible. The more specific the goal, the better the chance is to realize that goal. Vague goals are nothing more than wishes. It is as simple as the difference between "I want to lose weight" and "I want to lose twenty pounds." The second statement is a specific goal that can be measured as work toward it progresses.

Know exactly what is desired as a reward when the goal is achieved. If the goal is weight loss, perhaps the reward is being able to wear that dress featured in the store window. If the goal is learning how to swim, then maybe the goal is to swim in the ocean for the first time ever. Plan how this goal will be achieved. Think about the senses that will be used along the way and how they will make this progress easier or more difficult.

Visualize the plan and try to imagine any possible obstacles. That does not mean putting the obstacles in the path, but in being aware of the possibility that they might crop up and having a plan to defeat them. If the intended goal involves weight loss, what will be the plan for coping with the buffet during the holiday season? If the goal is to complete classes online then what happens if the internet goes out or the computer crashes? It is necessary to have a back-up plan to deal with life's little emergencies.

What will be used for markers along the way to track progress toward the goal? If the goal is weight loss, then perhaps a wall chart with every five pounds lost marked in red. Perhaps a drawing of a thermometer, with the goal being the mercury bulb at the top, and the thermometer is filled in gradually with every pound lost. Have a system in place to track these milestones.

Be aware that working toward any goal might come with negatives attached. Changing careers will most certainly mean a change in income. What if the career change means moving to another state? Is that a viable option? An extreme amount of weight loss will mean constantly refreshing the wardrobe. It is important to be aware of anything that might be seen as a negative effect of reaching the goal. These must be acceptable or the goal will need to be changed.

And when little distractions occur along the way, do not let them cancel out any progress that has already been made. Life happens. All roads have bumps in them. Even Shakespeare knew that no matter how good the plan was, it might not work. So acknowledge the fact that little bumps in the road will happen and have a plan to overcome them. Maybe it was a temporary lapse in judgement. Maybe it is a sign that the current path needs to take a bit of a different direction. The choice is solely up to the person who set the goal and created the path. And when the goal is reached, so will be the desired outcome.

MIND CONTROL TECHNIQUES

M ind control involves using influence and persuasion to
change the behaviors and beliefs in someone. That someone
might be the person themselves or it might be someone else. Mind
control has also been referred to as brainwashing, thought reform,
coercive persuasion, mental control, and manipulation, just to name a
few. Some people feel that everything is done by manipulation. But if
that is true to be believed, then important points about manipulation
will be lost. Influence is much better thought of as a mental
continuum with two extremes. One side has influences that are
respectful and ethical and work to improve the individual while
showing respect for them and their basic human rights. The other
side contains influences that are dark and destructive that work to
remove basic human rights from a person, such as independence, the
ability for rational thought, and sometimes their total identity.

When thinking of mind control, it is better to see it as a way to
use influence on other people that will disrupt something in them,
like their way of thinking or living. Influence works on the very basis
of what makes people human, such as their behaviors, beliefs, and
values. It can disrupt the very way they chose personal preferences or

make critical decisions. Mind control is nothing more than using words and ideas to convince someone to say or do something they might never have thought of saying or doing on their own.

There are scientifically proven methods that can be used to influence other people. Mind control has nothing to do with fakery, ancient arts, or even magical powers. Real mind control really is the basis of a word that many people hate to hear. That word is marketing. Many people hate to hear that word because of the negative connotations associated with it. When people hear "marketing," they automatically assume that it refers to those ideas taught in business school. But the basis of marketing is not about deciding which part of the market to target or deciding which customers will likely buy this product. The basis of marketing is one very simple word. That word is "YES."

If a salesperson asks a regular customer to write a brief endorsement of the product they buy, hopefully, they will say yes. If someone asks their significant other to take some of the business cards to pass out at work, hopefully, they will say yes. If you write any kind of blog and ask another blogger to provide a link to yours on their blog, hopefully, they will say yes. When enough people say yes, the business or blog will begin to grow. With even more yesses, it will continue to grow and thrive. This is the very simple basis of marketing. Marketing is nothing more than using mind control to get other people to buy something or to do something beneficial for someone else. And the techniques can easily be learned.

The first technique in mind control is to tell people what you want them to want. Never tell people to think it over or take some time. That is a definite mind control killer. People already have too much going on in their minds. When they are told to think something over they will not. It will be forgotten, and then it will never happen. This has nothing to do with being stupid or lazy and everything to do with just being way too busy.

So the best strategy is to take the offensive and think for them. Everything must be explained in the beginning. Never assume that the other blogger will automatically understand the benefits of adding a link will be for them. Do not expect anyone to give a demonstration blindly. And merely asking for a testimonial, while it might garner an appositive response, probably will not garner a well-formed testimonial to the product. Instead, be prepared to explain the blog, show examples, and offer compelling reasons why this merger will be a benefit to both parties. Have the demonstration laid out in great detail with notes on what to say when and visuals to go along with the notes, so all the other person has to do is present the information. Offer the customer a few variations of testimonials that have already been received and ask them to choose one and personalize it a bit. Always be specific in explaining what is desired. Explain why it is desired. Show how this will work. Tell the person how to do it and why they should do it. If done correctly it will feel exactly like one friend advising another friend on which is the best path to take. And the answer will be yes simply because saying yes makes so much sense.

Think of the avalanche. Think of climbing all the way to the top of the highest mountain ever. Now, at the top, think of searching for the biggest heaviest boulder that exists on the mountain. Now, picture summoning up superhuman strength to push this boulder, dislodging it from the place it has rested for years and years. Once this boulder is loosened, it rolls easily over the edge of the cliff, crashing into thousands of other boulders on its way down the mountain, taking half of the mountain with it in a beautiful cascade of rocks and dirt. Imagine sitting there smiling cheerfully at the avalanche that was just created.

Marketing and mind control are very like creating an avalanche. Getting the first person to answer yes might be difficult. But each subsequent yes will be easier and easier. And always start at the top, never the bottom. Starting at the top is definitely more difficult, and it is more likely to come with more negative responses than positive responses in the beginning. But starting at the top also yields a much greater reward when the avalanche does begin. And the results will be far greater than beginning at the bottom of the mountain. Yes, the small rock is easier to push over. Then it can be built upon by pushing over another small rock, then another. This way can work, but it will take much longer than being successful at the top. No one ever went fishing for the smallest fish in the pond or auditioned for the secondary role just to be safe. Everyone wants that top prize. Do not be afraid to go for it.

On the other hand, never ask for the whole boulder the first time. Ask for part of it. This may seem directly contradictory but it is not. Always start with a small piece. Make the beginning easier for everyone to see. Let other people use their own insight to see the end result. When the first bit goes well, then gradually ask for more and more and more.

Think of writing a guest spot for someone else who has their own blog. By sending in the entire manuscript first, there is a greater risk of rejection. Begin small. Send them a paragraph or two discussing them the idea. Then make an outline of the idea and send that in an email. Then write the complete draft you would like them too use and send it along. When asking a customer for a testimonial, start by asking for a few lines in an email. Then ask the customer to expand those few lines into a testimonial that covers at least half a typed page. Soon the customer will be ready for an hour-long webcast extolling the virtues of the product and your great customer service skills.

Everything must have a deadline that really exists. The important word here is the word 'real'. Everyone has heard the salesperson who said to decide quickly because the deal might not be available later or another customer was coming in and they might get it. That is a total fabrication and everyone knows it to be true. There are no impending other customers and the deal is not going to disappear. There is no real sense of urgency involved. But everyone does it. There are too many situations where people are given a totally fake deadline by someone who thinks it will instill a great sense of urgency for completion of the task. It is not only totally not effective but completely unneeded. It is a simple matter to create true urgency. Only leave free things available for a finite amount of time. When asking customers for testimonials be certain to mention the last possible day for it to be received to be able to be used. Some people will be unable to assist, but having people unable to participate is better than never being able to begin.

Always give before you receive. And do not ever think that giving is fifty-fifty. Always give much more than is expected in return. Before asking for a testimonial from a satisfied customer, be sure to make numerous acts of exceptional customer service. Before asking a blog writer for a link, link theirs to yours many times. This is not about helping someone out so they will help you. This is all about being so totally generous that the person who is asked for the favor cannot possibly say no. It might mean extra work, but that is how to influence other people.

Always stand up for something that is much bigger than average. Do not just write another blog on how to do something. Use an important issue to take a stand and defend the stance with unbeatable logic and fervent passion. Do not just write a how-to manual. Choose a particular idea and sell people on it, using examples of other people with the same idea living the philosophy.

Never feel shame. This does not mean being extremely extroverted to the point of silliness or having a total lack of conscience in business dealings. In the case of mind control shamelessness refers to a total complete belief that this course of action is the best possible course and everyone will benefit greatly from it. This is about writing the best possible blog ever and believing that everyone needs to read it to be able to improve their lives. It is about believing in a particular product so deeply that the feeling is that everyone will benefit from using it. It is knowing deep inside that this belief is the most correct belief ever and everyone should believe it.

Mind control uses the idea that someone's decisions and emotions can be controlled using psychological means. It is using powers of negotiation or mental influence to ensure the outcome of the interaction is more favorable to one person over the other. This is basically what marketing is: convincing someone to do something particular or buy something in particular. Being able to control someone else's mind merely means understanding the power of human emotion and being able to play upon those emotions. It is easier to have a mental impact on people if there is a basic understanding of human emotions. Angry people will back down when the subject of their anger is not afraid. Angry people feed upon the fear of others. Guilt is another great motivator. Making someone feel guilty for not thinking or feeling, in the same manner, is a wonderful way to get them to give in. Another way to use mind control over someone is to point out how valuable they are to the situation. Controlling the mind of another does not mean depriving them of free will and conscious thought. It means knowing what to say to impact the other person so profoundly they cannot see any other way to go but the one proposed.

MIND CONTROL WITH NLP FOR LOVE
AND RELATIONSHIPS

People are often a product of their environment, whether they want to be or not. The way people are raised directly affects the way they act in later life. Someone who is raised by alcoholics has a greater chance of becoming alcoholics in adult life, or they may choose never to drink at all. People who are raised in a house where everything is forbidden may cut loose and go a bit crazy when they are finally out on their own. People who are raised in total disorganization may grow up to be totally obsessive about household cleanliness.

Nurture affects people in other, less severe ways, too. Many people believe that Mom's meatloaf is the absolute best and no other recipe exists. People come from different religious and economic backgrounds. People have different beliefs about what is good and bad, what is acceptable and unacceptable. The problem comes when two people are trying to have a relationship, but neither wants to change their way of thinking. When that happens there is no relationship. There are just two people living together under the same roof.

Achieving success in love is just like achieving success in anything else. It is mostly a function of developing good relationships with other people in order to be better able to influence them. Those people who are successful in creating and keeping good, mutually satisfactory relationships with others usually enjoy much more success than people who do not do this. The ability to grow and maintain satisfactory relationships is a trait that is easier for some people. But even if the ability does not come naturally it is easy enough to learn. And Neuro-Linguistic Programming (NLP) makes this skill easier to learn by offering tools and ideas to enable almost anyone to learn the ability to develop great relationships.

People never stop communicating with each other. Any type of social contact is done with some form of communication. Even if there is no actual speaking, there is communicating. If a couple has an argument and stops talking to one another, they are now using frustration and anger to communicate in silence. Teenagers who close themselves off in their rooms and refuse to speak to the remainder of the family are silently communicating their desire to be left alone. Even in situations that are more neutral people continue to communicate with looks, sighs, and body language.

Becoming more aware of this will bring a hugely different perspective on personal relationships. A great deal of the actual communication between two people is unconscious and not verbal. People send out unconscious signals all the time to other people without even realizing they are doing it. The first most important step in improving relationships with others is to understand the ways people communicate without speaking and to become aware of these habits when they happen. Becoming better aware of these habits is a total life changer. Even if no other changes are made. Becoming better aware of the proper way to interact with others in life will make a huge impact on the quality of personal relationships.

People usually think their own opinion is right, that their own opinion is the best one there is in existence. NLP teaches us that humans see all experiences from behind a group of filters such as things that are expected and values that have been learned. These filters have been developed over a lifetime of learning. Once this is understood and accepted, it is infinitely easier to form an understanding of what drives the behavior of other people. Other people act in ways that may be quite different. People look at the world through lenses that see things differently. Other people have a different mental model of the world or they may travel on a different internal path.

In NLP, people are reminded that traveling the map is not the exact territory. Everyone has their own map. A normal course of action highly defends the home map. Instead, NLP guides people to try to understand the maps other people use on their travels through the world, and to make every attempt to learn from the differences in travel maps.

People who truly want to control a situation will learn to behave with the most flexibility. Think of the situations seen in nature. Plants and animals that are most likely to survive are those that are able to quickly adapt to the situation. Plants grow in the desert because they have adapted to the lack of water and are able to survive on very little. Small rodents survive a harsh winter by storing food to eat when there is not readily available food. Animals in the Arctic Circle will fatten up during the fall in order to have fat stores to feed them during the lean months of hibernation. This line of thought is also applicable to humans.

Using the map of the personal world analogy, think of it this way: people who can easily switch their thoughts among different world maps will easily be able to communicate with many different groups of people. These people will be much more effective at creating and maintaining meaningful relationships with others. Those people who only see and understand one method of behavior or one distinct way of viewing the world will eventually be left behind. They will become isolated as situations in the world change until they are no longer relevant in the real world.

When others do not understand the message, it is automatically seen to be their own fault. A person gives a message and expects that it will be easily understood by everyone else. This is often not the way things work. Using NLP gives a new perspective on this understanding. NLP teaches that it is the responsibility of the person sending the message to communicate in a way that the message can be easily understood. If it is not easily understood, the fault lies with the sender, not with the receiver. This all goes back to the idea of flexibility. If a person wants someone else to get the message, that person needs to speak in the other person's language. It is necessary to know exactly what the other person feels, what their concerns are, and what they are driven by. A person needs to set aside their own view of the world as much as possible. Communication is the responsibility of the communicator; if the message is not received, then it probably needs to be communicated in a different manner.

When babies are learning to walk and they fall over they usually cry. This is how they communicate with the people around them. Experience has taught them that if they cry someone will come to help them. Adults behave in much the same way but they do not indulge in kicking and screaming—usually. Adults learn more complex ways to behaving, hopefully, more sophisticated ways of getting their point across. But the underlying principle is still the same. People will believe in a way they feel will bring about the best results. But when using NLP, the goal is to make all behaviors have an intention that is positive.

It is much easier to develop meaningful relationships if time is taken to understand exactly why people act the way they do. People should not use their own point of view when doing this. People must look at the point of view of other people and try to see things the way they do. Then it will be possible to offer other people new ideas in order to help them develop a behavior that is more productive. People make the best possible choices they can, based on the information they already possess. Sometimes the best alternative someone can offer another person is a new way of looking at a situation. It is never helpful to constantly solve someone else's problems for them. This practice does not work forever. The best method is to give people the tools they need to be able to solve their own problems. Doing this will also help to strengthen relationships between people.

The real idea behind NLP is taking responsibility for personal actions. NLP tells us that people see life as being a function of either cause or effect. People operate from one perspective or the other. If people see themselves operating from a cause position, they see themselves as totally in control of a situation and able to manipulate the situation to control the outcome. When people operate from the idea of the effect, they easily blame other people or life circumstances for their problems. There is always a valid reason to justify why they are not happy or healthy or successful. The real truth is that no matter what opinion people operate from they are always in control of the situation and the choice of which point of view to operate from.

When a relationship is not going well, for whatever reason, the best choice is always to consider personal behavior and how it can be changed. If operating from the position of the cause, then the person has the ability to make improvements in the situation. This is done by understanding the other person's point of view by hearing what they are really saying and learning to communicate with others on a level they can communicate easily on.

Remember that people will do the best they know how to do with the tools they have to work with. Personal resources determine personal behavior. If people had different tools or a different point of view they might act in a different way. People should never be labeled based on their behavior. This perspective will never help with the development of great relationships. Behavior can change as people learn new skills and grow and develop. Sometimes relationships are labeled as stagnant or bad. Sometimes relationships are unproductive and unfulfilling. But these relationships can be turned around and saved by both parties learning to take responsibility for the situation and learning to be proactive in their behavior. Everyone is capable of accomplishing wonderful things. Everyone is able to enjoy a world full of fulfilment and success. The fact that everyone is responsible for their own destiny is often a frightening thought.

Another tactic that can be effectively used to improve interpersonal relationships is to work to find some form of common ground. The first step is to ask questions about general topics that the other person seems to have an interest in. This will provide a basis for understanding the other person. Then more in-depth topics can be discussed. This is a good method for learning about common values and principles that can be used as the basis for a meaningful relationship. It is also a good idea to ask questions that will give more information into the thought processes of the other person. Stay away from specific ideas. Instead, talk in generalities that will give more of the big picture.

Once there is a common ground to work on, then the other tactics of the NLP method will be able to be used to intensify the feelings between the two people in the relationship, including the feelings of love that pass between them. Love is nothing more than an intense reaction of fondness for a particular person. Love is impossible to define because everyone has a different view of what makes a person loveable.

All the methods of NLP can be used to strengthen the love between two people. The first thing to do is to admit that everyone has a different idea of love and what it means, based on how they were raised and what they saw growing up. Differences will not matter as long as two people truly love one another and want to make the relationship work. Understand the different maps people travel on. Remember that the way people behave will often depend on the path they travel in life. Also, remember that people look at the world differently. Everyone's life experiences will cause them to look at life differently. Everyone's reaction to love and affection will be clouded by the filters they are looking through. By understanding this, it is easier to communicate with loved ones.

Also, keep in mind that the way a relationship is approached will greatly determine how the relationship will turn out. People who can approach a relationship with caring and thoughtfulness will end up with a much better relationship than people who demand their own way in the relationship.

THE MOST POWERFUL
MIND-POWER TOOL

Humans spend countless hours seeking new ways to work just about anything. Through endless hours of research, they pour over books and journals looking for the message that will tell them the secret to harnessing mind power. Many never realize that the most powerful mind power tool is already on board and just aching to be used. It is the human brain, the mind itself.

Every time a person practices a new habit or thinks a new thought, they make a new pathway in the brain. Every time the habit is used, or the idea is thought, the nerve pathway becomes even stronger. The human brain is wired at birth to be an efficient machine and it is ready, from birth, to make an ever increasing amount of nerve pathways and to strengthen the pathways that are used the most.

Sometimes thoughts and habits need to be changed for the improvement of the person. When people decide that they would like to make a change in their lives, there will be a period of adjustment. This is true whether the change is mental, emotional, or physical. During this period of adjustment, there will be some level of discomfort. When a habit or a thought is already formed, it has made its own path in the brain. When a stimulus is seen or heard, the message travels along the preset nerve pathway to the spot in the brain that controls that thought or habit. In order to change a thought or a habit, it is necessary for the nerve path to be changed. Until the nerve path is changed, the old nerve path will remain in the brain. The discomfort comes from the brain trying to automatically access the old pathway and the new pathway at the same time. This is painful for the brain to do.

It is easy to become frustrated when the brain goes back to its old patterns of thought and habit. Never fall into the habit of placing blame on a lack of willpower. Willpower has nothing to do with it. It is a very difficult thing to override preset pathways in the brain. The brain is a very powerful tool. When will power fails and mistakes happen, remember to use kindness and compassion in dealing with the failure. The brain is very efficient at doing what it does. The only way to change the pathways in the brain is to keep working on new pathways that will eventually obliterate the old, undesirable ones.

The brain needs a clear understanding that changes are about to take place and new pathways are about to be laid down. Remind the brain that new habits and new thoughts will be replacing the old ones. Blaming failure on a lack of will power is a self-defeating statement. The process of making new nerve paths in the brain takes hard work and time. It will help to keep reminding oneself of the impending change. By doing this over and over, it makes the process no longer about possible character flaws. The focus is now put on the habit of thought that is being built.

Is it possible to build new nerve pathways in the brain? Yes, it is possible, and it can be done. If more proof is needed, just compare the adult brain to the baby's brain. Every current habit and thought a person has is the direct result of having spent time practicing them over and over until they created a pathway in the brain. New pathways can be created. Think of it this way: they already have. The baby's brain has no idea of anything. It has no thoughts or habits. Every nerve path currently in the brain was practiced until it became a part of the brain. Think of the baby. The baby lies around day after day and does baby things. Then one day the baby notices the shiny rattle that mommy is waving in front of its little face. The baby wants the rattle. As the baby is waving its tiny arms around, the mommy puts the rattle close enough so the baby can touch it with its wavering hand. After a few of these sessions, the baby gets the idea that if the arm is in the air it can touch the rattle. A nerve pathway is beginning to grow. So the baby decides to lift its arm to actively reach for the rattle. The baby will be unsuccessful at first because the arms will wave wildly and will not connect with the rattle. One day, the baby will actually grab the rattle, and the nerve pathway is then complete.

While this may seem like a very simple example, it is exactly how nerve pathways are created in the brain. Every action, thought, or habit has its own nerve pathway. All pathways must be created. No one was born knowing to sit in front of the television and mindlessly eat dip with chips. No one was born lamenting the excess pounds they carry in strange places. No one was born hating their body. All behaviors are learned, good and bad. And the bad ones can be replaced with good ones.

So if the ability to program negative thoughts into the brain exists, then the ability to disrupt those negative thoughts with positive thoughts also exists. The brain can be reprogrammed. It is a powerful tool, and its main function is to turn thoughts into reality. The brain is always working, so why not use the power of the brain to benefit rather than harm? Just because a particular habit or thought has been around all forever does not mean it needs to stay. Use the power of the brain to choose new habits and thoughts to focus on and replace the old, negative thought pathways in the brain.

The new thought needs to be believable; the new habit needs to be doable. It does not real good to try to stick to a habit that is impossible to accomplish or to try to believe a thought that is unbelievable. After years of seeing the reality of an obese body, it would be nearly impossible to suddenly believe that the image in the mirror is that of a skinny person. But the brain will likely accept something that mentions learning to take care of the body or learning to accept the body in order to correct its flaws. The brain will turn a belief in reality. Believing a positive thought will lead to quite a different result than the ending where only negative thoughts are present.

Be prepared to repeat and repeat some more. The primary key to being able to make a new habit stay is repeating it constantly. The more a new, desirable habit is practiced, the more the brain begins to accept it. The nerve path becomes stronger every day. With constant practice, this new nerve path will become the path the brain will prefer to use, and the old one will cease to exist.

In any case, be sure to allow enough time to effectively create a change. Accept the starting point and constantly visualize the ending point. Accept the fact that the path to the goal of a new habit or thought will not be easy or perfect. The path will almost never travel in a straight line. Sometimes people fall completely off the path, and that is okay too. Just get back up and get back on. Do not get sidetracked by the idea that this journey will be easy and carefree because it will not be. Just keep thinking of the new nerve pathway that will be created by the new thought or habit and it will eventually become a reality.

Most of the pathways in the brain are stored in the subconscious mind. This is the part of the mind that is always working without always being thought of. Think of learned skills like tying shoes, zipping a coat, and pouring milk into a glass. These were all learned behavior whose nerve pathways are firmly set in the subconscious part of the mind. This part of the brain is the bank of data for all life functions.

The communication between the conscious mind and the unconscious mind works in both directions. Whenever a person has a memory, and emotion, or an idea, it is rooted in the subconscious mind and translated to the conscious mind through mind power. The subconscious has the power to control just about anything a human does regularly.

For example, during meditation steady, deep breathing is usually practiced. The control of the breath is brought from the subconscious mind and given to the conscious mind to tell it to control the breathing. Once a pattern of deep steady breathing is begun by the conscious mind, the subconscious mind takes over and keeps the set rhythm going until it is told to stop. This is done by a conscious end to the deep breathing or an encounter with an outside stimulus like stress. The subconscious mind also processes the great wealth of information received daily and only passes along to the conscious mind those things that are necessary for the brain to remember.

When sending thoughts from the conscious mind to the subconscious mind, the brain will only send those thoughts that are attached to great emotion. The only thoughts that remain in the subconscious are those that are kept there with strong emotions. Unfortunately, the brain does not know the difference between positive emotions and negative emotions. Any strong emotion will work. Both negative emotions and positive emotions can be quite strong. Also, unfortunately, negative emotions tend to be stronger than positive emotions.

Step one in learning to use the power of the subconscious part of the mind will be to eliminate any thoughts that come with negative emotions. Also, negative mental comments will also need to cease. Fears will usually come true, specifically because they are drowning in negative emotion. This is why negative ideas need to be eliminated because they can be very harmful roadblocks on the road to harnessing brain power.

One best practice to use to get rid of negative thoughts is to counter them with positive thoughts. This will take time and practice, but it is a very powerful and useful technique. Whenever a negative thought pops in the conscious mind, immediately counter it with a positive thought that is dripping with strong emotion. The actual truth will come out somewhere in between the two thoughts.

Another way to counter negative emotions is to delete them, just like using a remote control. When a negative thought comes into the conscious mind, imagine destroying it. Imagine writing that thought on paper and burning it. Imagine pointing a remote control at the thought and pressing a huge delete button. Whatever form used to imagine deleting the thought, the important thing is to get rid of it before it can take hold in the subconscious mind.

Find something energizing and use it to reach a goal. Those things that are found to be energizing bring boundless energy to positive thoughts. It is often necessary to invent motivation, at least in the beginning, to learn to create new habits and thoughts. But with a bit of practice and a lot of positive thought, new positive habits will soon be burned into the subconscious mind and the old negative thoughts and habit will fade away.

ASSUMING SUCCESS

S uccess and failure are both normal parts of life. Unfortunately, fearing failure is a huge cloud that hangs over good judgement and can lead to extremely flawed thought patterns. When failure is seen as a possible outcome, then people automatically set their expectations lower. Working with lowered expectations means that there is not as far to fall when failure does happen. There are moments in life when it makes sense to intentionally set sights lower in order to minimize risks. But these moments are few and far between. People who doubt the possibility of success will automatically increase the possibility of less personal growth or eventual failure. Really the only way to guarantee future growth is to look at all the options with the idea of eventual success in mind, not in an arrogant manner but with quiet confidence in a successful outcome.

Keeping this attitude will be especially difficult in the beginning of this process when no positive outcomes have been proven. It is far too easy to just talk about success when failure is the only outcome known. The key is to practice positive thinking. The next time it is time to make an important decision to try to imagine a positive outcome. Try to imagine that failure is not an option or even something to worry about.

Assuming success means making good choices that will point toward success. Spend time on those things that matter and leave the unimportant things behind. The focus should always be on the big picture and never on moments where gratification is instant. Assuming success will also mean being ready to accept the responsibility for success and being accountable to use it correctly. It involves doing what is right and not just taking the easiest path to completion. Always be prepared to follow the path to the decided goal.

People who assume success are willing to give up the idea of staying within the zone of comfort. Dark fears must be faced in order to be conquered. Be prepared to put safety and security on the line in a quest for success that might mean taking huge personal risks. Safety nets are always nice to have but they are so *safe*. Safety does not often lead to success. The path to success is filled with great risks. Be prepared to have the courage to create a personal path and be prepared to walk it no matter what happens.

All things take courage when the ultimate quest is success. Achieving success takes hard work, perseverance, and great discipline. Persuasion is important too. It will often be necessary to engage others to assist with the travels on the way to the goal of success. Do not be afraid to use the powers of persuasion when needed to achieve these goals. And use mind control to enable the making of good choices. Luck will not enable anyone to achieve success; only hard work with good choices will take the path to success.

Each day is full of decisions that might affect the future of life as it is known now. Every day people must choose what to do and what things to say. Choices must be made to either be well behaved or to misbehave. Every day of every life is potentially filled with choices to be made that might actually affect the very outcome of life in the future. The burning question is whether the choices made today will lead toward future success. The answer should be a completely honest one because it is vital to the success of future decisions.

Making good choices is never easy. Good choices are difficult ones. But it is the good choices that will eventually lead to success. The first good choices are the hardest ones, especially if making good choices has not been a regular habit in the past. But each subsequent good choice will cause making good choices to become easier.

Some people will spend the whole of their lives trying to figure out how to be successful. Personal success is an achievable goal for anyone who truly wants to achieve success. Most people do want to be independent financially, to enjoy a wonderful career, and to have a strong and satisfying home life. People want to know they are important, that they matter to someone else, at least one someone else. Almost everyone wants to do at least one wonderful thing in their life. This is how most people measure the extent of success.

And achieving success is not dependent on built-in ability, intelligence, or background. Success does not care who a person knows. Everyone has the ability to do wonderful things in life and to achieve success. The key is to assume that success is the ultimate goal and no other potential outcome will be acceptable.

Do not be afraid to question the path of life if it is not leading toward success. It is quite alright to ask questions of other people if it is necessary to learn how to reach success. Just never assume that someone else's path will be the only one that exists. Everyone must choose a personal path to success. Everyone must define the idea of success for themselves. Take in advice from others and use the tips and tricks that make sense. Discard the rest. Only do what feels tight and acceptable.

The first goal achieved is perhaps the most important goal on the road to success. The first goal proves that goals can be achieved. The first goal will begin to program the brain to accept the idea of success and to develop new pathways that will facilitate becoming successful. People will only learn to succeed by achieving success. The more goals that are achieved, the more goals people want to achieve. Success builds confidence that leads to more goal achievement that leads to more success that leads to more confidence. It grows in an ever-widening circle.

The only real limit on success is a personal limit. With the true success, the sky is the limit. Once the decision to push aside limits of the mind has been made, then anything can be achieved. If goal accomplishment is approached with a completely open heart and mind then anything can be achieved. Once the habit of achieving goals is begun, there really is no limit on personal success. As long as progress is not halted, then success is practically guaranteed.

Be prepared to chase success mercilessly. Success is a goal and a way of life. Once success is first achieved, it creates a burning desire for more success. Never be content to stop with just one success. Always strive for more success.

Realize that sometimes life flows a certain direction and that direction cannot be changed. There are times that life will get in the way of the pursuit of success. Recognize these moments for temporary distractions and not permanent set-in-stone ways of life. All life choices will go off the rails at times. The path to achieving a goal can be disrupted by unexpected roadblocks. Life happens. Never lose sight of success or allow these interruptions to permanently derail the success train.

Always try to set goals that are realistic and achievable. No one can possibly hope to lose one hundred pounds overnight, or even in one month. That is not a realistic goal. Instead, be prepared to set many small goals that will lead to the achievement of the ultimate goal. There is no miracle transformation in sight. But, through hard work and attention to detail goal will be achieved and success will be assured.

Remember to stay positive. Positive feelings will enable the mind to create greater thought patterns that will lead to the brain making more connections between thoughts and ideas. Connections that are new and fresh to the mind can easily lead to a rush of creative thoughts. These creative thoughts can easily ferment in the mind and lead to wonderful new thoughts in the future. Learn to relax. Anger and stress are definite creativity killers. Using relaxation techniques will recharge the brain and relax the nerves to allow positive thoughts to flow through more freely. Before pondering any problem, take a few minutes to breathe deeply and relax.

Do not make the mistake of being too nice when traveling the path to success. Of course, everyone wants to treat themselves nicely, even if it is only occasionally, but do not make the mistake of being too nice to the mind. Pamper the body and work the mind. Of course, making extremely negative personal comments is never a good idea. The comments like "You are so fat" and "You will never amount to anything" are definitely self-defeating. But do not be too easy on that person inside who craves success. Being too nice can have negative consequences. Being too nice usually means not pushing oneself to one's ultimate potential. Failure is okay because it is expected. Thoughts like these will never lead to ultimate success. It is okay to be a little tough every now and then. No great goal was ever reached without a lot of sweat and agony. Be prepared to suffer. Suffering now just makes success all that much sweeter when it does arrive.

Success begins with a dream. Anything worth having is worth dreaming about. Open the heart and the mind to the possibility of success. Take the time to wonder how life will change when success is achieved. Think only positive thoughts. Negative thoughts are too discouraging. Dream of all the possibilities that come with real success. Keep the dream alive, fan its flames every time it seems to be growing cold. Never let the dream go away.

The dream of success needs to be big, huge, enormous. The dream of success needs to feel much bigger than anything that might be achieved in this life. In addition to feeling really intense, it also needs to be something that is believable. The dream must be seen as something that it is possible to achieve if everything falls into place correctly. If hard work if offered, if other people lend a hand, if certain life events happen at the right time, then the dream of success is one that can be achieved.

Everyone who is able to achieve great things is able to see those great things in their minds. They can picture themselves wallowing in success, whatever success means to them. Imagining a successful outcome makes achieving a successful outcome much more realistic. A basketball player will imagine the ball going through the net with every shot. A pageant queen will imagine the crown on her head. A jockey will imagine his horse crossing the finish line first. Imagining something to be a reality is the first step into making it a reality. And creating reality is the first step toward assuming success and all the perks that come with it.

Success depends greatly on mind control and assuming success is just another way to practice mind control to create a goal of success. Success itself is both a goal and a way of life. It is possible to program the mind to focus more completely on the idea of achieving success. Remember that every habit and every thought, both positive and negative, has its own pathway in the mind. All these pathways are created through repeated practice of these habits and thoughts. Negative thoughts will need to be replaced by positive thoughts. Negative habits will need to be replaced by positive habits. All negativity will create roadblocks to true success. The pathways of negative thoughts and habits will be eliminated by the practice of positive thoughts and habits. Success is one of these positive habits.

CONCLUSION

Thank you for making it through to the end of *Manipulation: Techniques in Dark Psychology, Influencing People with Persuasion, NLP, and Mind Control*. Let's hope it was informative and able to provide you with all of the tools you need to achieve your goals whatever they may be.

The next step is to make the conscious decision that success is the way of life you want to live. Read through this book carefully, making notes if needed. Take advantage of the information contained in this book. Pay careful attention to the sections on using mind control and developing new thought patterns in the mind. These sections will be especially helpful in learning to create a goal that will lead to the achievement of success, whatever success is in your life.

Finally, if you found this book useful in any way, a review on Amazon is always appreciated!

CPSIA information can be obtained
at www.ICGtesting.com
Printed in the USA
LVHW082235230122
709180LV00031B/732

9 781087 861968